BEHIND THE WHEEL

Great Road Racing Drivers

BEHIND THE WHEEL

Great Road Racing Drivers

by Robert B. Jackson

illustrated with photographs

71- 5037

NEW YORK | HENRY Z. WALCK, INC.

796.7   Jackson, Robert B.
   J   Behind the wheel: great road racing
         drivers. Walck, 1971
           56p. illus.

           Concise biographies of twenty-two
         of the greatest international drivers
         of our time.

         1. Automobile drivers   I. Title

THE PHOTOGRAPH OF JUAN FANGIO ON PAGE 31 WAS SUPPLIED BY UNITED
PRESS INTERNATIONAL. OTHER PHOTOGRAPHS ARE BY THE AUTHOR.

COPYRIGHT © 1971 BY ROBERT B. JACKSON
ALL RIGHTS RESERVED
ISBN: 0-8098-2076-5
LIBRARY OF CONGRESS CATALOG CARD NUMBER: 77-145416
PRINTED IN THE UNITED STATES OF AMERICA

Contents

1 / Behind the Wheel

Thundering down long straights at two hundred miles an hour, sweeping through bending turns only inches from disaster, wheel to wheel they race. International road racing is the most demanding form of automotive competition; and the men who race the road courses of the world are among the most exciting in sport.

They are courageous, capable of intense concentration, and have split-second reflexes. They are masters of gear-shifting and braking, and they can follow the fastest possible route through a succession of twisting curves in precisely the same way lap after lap.

Road racing is thus more complex than either drag or track racing. It is also more widespread. Starting in Europe shortly after automobiles were first developed there, the sport is now highly popular in other parts of the world as well. As a result the important road races are run under international rules, and both cars and drivers come from a number of different countries.

In recent years British drivers have been most prominent; and one chapter of this book contains profiles of several of the best-known. Their influence has spread to Australia and New Zealand, and another chapter deals with the stars of road racing who have come from there.

The popularity of road racing has also zoomed in this country recently. An obscure amateur pursuit during the nineteen-forties, U. S. road racing grew into a big-time professional sport in the sixties. This great expansion has helped create a group of American drivers who can hold their own with the best in international competition; and the last chapter tells about them.

Many of these top-flight road racing drivers started their careers with street-type sports cars or sedans in low-pressure amateur events. Others followed the European pattern and began with motorcycle racing or automobile hillclimbs in which single cars race the clock up a winding mountain road.

As the drivers move up to larger and faster cars, the big league for sports car racing is the International Manufacturers' Championship. This annual series of ten or so events is held on such courses as Sebring, Florida, Le Mans, France, the Nürburgring in Germany, Brands Hatch, England, the Targa Florio course in Sicily and Watkins Glen, New York. The races are long-distance endurance contests lasting as long as twenty-four hours and requiring a pair of alternating drivers. The automobiles are mostly specially designed and built sports / racing cars rather than everyday mass-production sports cars like those on the street.

International rules specify that sports/racing cars have doors, enclosed wheels, headlights and space for a passenger. The intention is to keep sports racers at least something like sports cars of the street; and even space for luggage was called for in the past.

None of these restrictions applies to formula cars, however. Formula cars, so-called because of the formula or set of rules that governs each class, are the ultimate form of road racing machinery. They are stripped, single-seater, all-out racing cars. Light but extremely powerful, they are the most difficult of all racing cars to drive at their limit.

There are three international groups of formula cars, ranging from Formula Three, the slowest, to Formula One, the fastest. The World Championship of road racing is determined each year by a points system based on the finishing positions in about a dozen championship

Grand Prix drivers are the most skillful of road racing competitors; and here are four of the best at the start of the 1968 U.S. Grand Prix. Numbers 10 and 12 are Briton Graham Hill and Italian-American Mario Andretti in Lotuses, Number 6 is New Zealander Chris Amon in a Ferrari, and Number 15, the winner, is Scot Jackie Stewart in a Matra.

Formula One races. Because of this, Formula One competition is also called Grand Prix racing, Grand Prix meaning "great prize" in French. Each participating country is allowed one championship Grand Prix a year, and the Formula One calendar usually includes races at Monte Carlo, Zandvoort, Holland, Spa, Belgium, Monza, Italy, Watkins Glen and Mexico City, among others.

Not all factory teams race both sports and formula cars. Some drivers therefore contract with one manufacturer for two-seater racing and another for Grand Prix events. Others drive in only one category at a time; but in any case the goal for an aspiring young road racer is always a factory Formula One ride.

Drivers on their way up often compete in sports cars for a time, then spend a season or two in Formula Three before advancing to Formula Two. They frequently buy their own cars at first or drive those that are independently owned. Then, if they are good enough, they may be put under contract by one of the factory teams. The factory teams are nearly always fastest because they naturally save the best cars for themselves.

2 / *Australia and New Zealand*

Jack Brabham

When he retired at the end of the 1970 season, Jack Brabham had been racing longer than any other driver active in Formula One. Reporters usually referred to him as "The Old Man," and he once kidded them by walking to his Grand Prix car wearing a false beard and leaning on a jack handle as a cane.

He was born in a suburb of Sydney, Australia, in 1926; and his earliest memories include steering the family car from his father's lap. By the time he was twelve he could drive the car and his father's grocery trucks as well.

An accomplished mechanic in his teens, he next spent two years in the Royal Australian Air Force, then helped an American ex-serviceman build a midget racing car in Sydney. When his friend retired from driving, Jack took over behind the wheel and won four Australian championships in as many years.

Also successful in Australian hillclimbs and road racing, he moved to England for further experience in 1955. The following year he was asked to join the Cooper team, whose rear-engined cars were about to revolutionize automobile racing. Twice a World Champion with Cooper in 1959 and 1960, he drove to the championship again in 1966, this time in a car of his own manufacture, the only driver ever to do so.

He is often called "Black Jack" because of his dark hair, bushy eyebrows and fast-growing beard, as well as his grim expression when in the cockpit. He could also be recognized while driving by his silver helmet, hunched shoulders, and the way he slid the tail of his car wide in the turns—a cornering style he carried over from his midget-racing days.

Bruce McLaren

When New Zealander Bruce McLaren was a boy he took the engine of his model airplane apart so often he wore it out. In 1946, at the age of nine, a hip ailment put him in a hospital, where he remained for three years. The resulting limp kept him from playing most sports. His father, a garage owner who raced motorcycles and cars himself occasionally, then gave Bruce an elderly Austin Seven racing car as a form of therapy.

Bruce learned to drive the Austin in his Auckland backyard and entered his first event, a hillclimb, when he was fifteen. He won his class that first time out and gradually moved up to sports car and formula racing while in college. His performances were so promising that a group of New Zealand racing enthusiasts sent him to England on a motor-racing "scholarship" in 1958.

He became the number-two Cooper driver behind Jack Brabham in 1959 and won the first United States Grand Prix that December. When Jack left to build his own cars in 1962, Bruce took over as Cooper's Number One. Two years later he followed Jack's example again and also set up his own racing organization.

A capable builder and driver of Grand Prix automobiles, Bruce was especially interested in sports cars. Co-driver of the winning Fords at Le Mans (1966) and Sebring (1967), he also developed the invincible

14 /

McLaren sports / racing cars. These orange speedsters currently dominate the recently organized Canadian-American series, sweeping twenty-three races in a row at one point. Bruce was the Can-Am champion driver in both 1967 and 1969.

Quiet, unassuming and highly likeable, Bruce insisted on testing his own cars. He was killed in June of 1970 when a new-model Can-Am car went out of control at 180 miles an hour.

DENNY HULME

After leaving school Denny Hulme (born in 1936)
went to work in his father's garage in Te Puke, New
Zealand. Shortly afterwards he started racing MG's,
usually driving in his bare feet. As he progressed to
faster cars—and learned to wear driving shoes—he did
so well that he was sent to compete in Europe in 1960
by the same group that had sponsored Bruce McLaren
two years earlier.

By 1963 he had landed a ride in a factory Formula
Junior Brabham. (Formula Junior was an earlier version
of the current Formula Three, smallest and slowest of
the three top international single-seater classes.) Denny
stepped up to a Formula Two Brabham in 1964 and
graduated to a Formula One Brabham for several races
during 1964 and 1965.

He became Jack's regular second driver for both F1
and F2 in 1966 and also had great success racing a Lola
T70 sports car. In 1967 he won his first Grand Prix,
Monaco, and went on to beat his boss by five points for
the World Championship.

Denny also joined the newly formed McLaren Can-
Am team in 1967. There were twenty-three Can-Am
races in the three seasons that followed; and either Bruce
or Denny won twenty of them. Not only did one of the
New Zealanders usually win, the other nearly always

placed second. They ran one-two so often that other drivers called the series "The Bruce and Denny Show." Bruce was Can-Am champion in 1967 and 1969, Denny in 1968 and 1970.

Balding and long in the jaw, Denny is a steady but fast driver who is generally smiling and easygoing around the pits. Since 1968 he has also driven McLaren cars in Formula One.

CHRIS AMON

New Zealanders are often called kiwis after the nearly extinct bird that is found only there; and Chris Amon always has a kiwi painted on each side of his helmet. Born in Bulls, New Zealand, in 1943 to a rich farming family, Chris was already racing regularly before he was seventeen. Unlike many drivers, he could afford to buy his own cars to get started. One of the first was a big Grand Prix 250F Maserati, quite a handful for a rather slight teen-ager.

Chris was competing on the difficult road circuits of Europe by the time he was nineteen, the youngest driver ever to start a Grand Prix. During his first two seasons his cars were not the best; but in 1965 he drove a Ford GT-40 with Phil Hill (page 42) at Le Mans and also joined the McLaren team.

He won the famous twenty-four-hour French event the following year, sharing a Ford with Bruce McLaren. He signed with the well-known Italian Ferrari team in 1967, and won his very first event with them, the twenty-four-hour sports car race at Daytona, Florida. During the winter of 1968-69 he returned home and drove a single-seater Ferrari in the Tasman series, a group of formula races held annually in New Zealand and Australia. He ran away with the overall championship, winning four of the seven races and placing third twice.

Chris has yet to win a championship Grand Prix, however. A smooth and quick driver of great promise, he has also been one of the unluckiest, often having mechanical failures while leading a race. In 1970 he switched to the English March team for its first season, then moved to the French Matra organization in 1971.

3 / Great Britain

STIRLING MOSS

Stirling Moss entered almost five hundred events during his brilliant career and won the amazing total of 194. Stirling was born in 1931, the son of a British dentist who had raced in his youth (including twice at Indianapolis) and a mother who had competed in amateur motor sports. He started winning behind the wheel with hillclimbs when he was eighteen.

Following several successful seasons in a variety of English sports and formula cars, Stirling drove Italian Maseratis in Grand Prix competition during 1954 and gained an international reputation. In 1955 he was asked to join the German Mercedes-Benz team, then the dominant force in road racing. As their second driver he learned much from Mercedes's Number One, the great Juan Fangio (page 30). He also won one of his greatest races in 1955, averaging nearly one hundred

miles an hour over a thousand miles of Italian public
roads in the Mille Miglia.

When Mercedes withdrew from racing, Fangio joined
Ferrari and Moss returned to Maserati. The pair then
became road racing's top rivals until Fangio retired in
1958, leaving Moss as the acknowledged master. Stirling
was never World Champion, however, mostly because
he preferred to race British cars at a time when they
were not yet the equal of those from other countries. His
two outstanding Grand Prix victories were at Monte
Carlo and the Nürburgring of Germany in 1961. In both
races he drove an independent Lotus against more
powerful factory teams. Retired since a bad crash in
1962, he remains knowledgeable and articulate about
the sport in his many public appearances.

Jim Clark

Juan Fangio himself once called Jim Clark of Scotland the greatest of all Grand Prix competitors; and many experts have since agreed. Jim died in 1968 at the peak of his career when his Lotus unaccountably left the road during a Formula Two race in Germany; but he had already been World Champion twice (1963 and 1965) and won more Grands Prix (twenty-five) than any other driver.

Born in 1936, Jim grew up on a large cattle and sheep farm in Duns. His parents did not entirely approve of his racing at first, and a group of young farmer friends helped Jim get started by sponsoring his car in several Scottish and English events. Starting with a Sunbeam and then progressively racing a Porsche, Jaguars and a Lotus Elite, he proved himself very fast indeed. Jim drove his first single-seater in December of 1959 and signed with Lotus as a Formula Junior and Formula Two driver in 1960. Within three months he was a regular Formula One driver as well, an exceptional achievement.

The Lotus Grand Prix car of the time, developed by manufacturer Colin Chapman (background of photo) was superior to those of other builders And since Jim had become virtually unbeatable barring mechanical problems, the team won a record-breaking seven Grands Prix in one season alone.

Equally fast on the track, Jim placed second his first time at Indianapolis and won the famous 500 in 1965. A small but vital man, he was surprisingly shy and reserved when out of the cockpit, avoiding public appearances as much as possible.

GRAHAM HILL

Tall, hawk-nosed and mustached, Graham Hill looks like Hollywood's idea of a racing driver. Widely known for his sharp wit, he is popular with spectators and drivers alike. A particular favorite in this country, he has won the United States Grand Prix three years in a row— 1963, 1964 and 1965—and the Indianapolis 500 in 1966. He has also been an unprecedented five-time winner at Monte Carlo.

Many racing drivers come from automotive backgrounds, but Hill's London stockbroker father did not even own a car. Born in 1929, Hill himself did not learn to drive until the age of twenty-four when he bought his first automobile. Shortly afterwards he answered an advertisement that offered four laps in a racing car for a pound and decided upon his present career. Working as a mechanic in exchange for occasional sports car rides put him on relief in the beginning; but he eventually joined Colin Chapman's Team Lotus, then in its early days.

Not very successful there, he moved to British Racing Motors in 1960, where his fortunes improved. He dueled Jim Clark for the championship throughout the 1962 season, speeding to victory and the championship in the last race of the season when Clark dropped out with engine trouble.

Hill returned to Lotus in 1967, winning the World Championship for the second time in 1968. He had a bad crash during the United States Grand Prix in 1969; but his great determination helped him to recover and drive for Rob Walker's independent team in 1970.

Like many of the other drivers, Graham is an accomplished pilot. He was also an enthusiastic rower in his youth, and the white stripes on his helmet represent the oars of the London Rowing Club.

JACKIE STEWART

Jackie Stewart has succeeded fellow Scot Jim Clark as the fastest driver in Formula One. Small and dark like Clark, Jackie has a burr in his speech that is even thicker; but he seems far more comfortable in the public eye. He talks and laughs easily with bright enthusiasm and favors Mod music, hair styles and clothes.

His father ran a garage, and an older brother, Jimmy, raced sports cars for some time. Jackie, who was born in 1939, worked in the garage after leaving school and devoted much of his spare time to becoming a championship trapshooter, barely missing making the Olympic team in 1960. About the same time he started racing under the name "A.N. Other," but his family soon found out about it anyway.

He won fourteen of twenty-three sports car races for Ecurie Ecosse, a Scottish team, and then signed with English lumber dealer Ken Tyrrell to drive in Formula Three. During 1964 he won every F3 race he started with the exception of two in which his car broke down. Skipping Formula Two entirely, he had his choice of Grand Prix teams in 1965; and he decided on British Racing Motors, serving his apprenticeship under Graham Hill.

In 1968 he rejoined Ken Tyrrell to drive an F1 Matra-Ford, a French car with an English engine. He swept six

of the eleven Grands Prix in 1969 with the Matra to become World Champion.

Jackie generally wears a black cap around the pits and the Stewart tartan on his helmet. He is very interested in improving course safety, particularly since his accident during the Belgian Grand Prix in which he was rescued from a gasoline-soaked car by Graham Hill.

JOHN SURTEES

John Surtees, born in 1934, was first a champion on two wheels. His father, a South London garage owner, was a motorcycle racer; and John had his first motorcycle when he was eleven. He and his father won their first race together (John in the sidecar) when John was fifteen.

Growing up to be one of the most successful cyclists ever to compete internationally, John was seven times a world champion during the late fifties. Searching for further challenge, John then made his auto racing debut in 1960, driving a Formula Junior Cooper belonging to Ken Tyrrell. Two months later he signed with Team Lotus and started his first Formula One race, the Grand Prix of Monaco at Monte Carlo.

John drove Coopers and Lolas for Bowmaker-Yeoman Racing during his second and third seasons, then switched to Ferrari of Italy. He won his first Grand Prix at the Nürburgring in 1963 and became World Champion in 1964. Very much his own man he moved to Cooper-Maserati in 1966, the Japanese Honda team in 1967, British Racing Motors in 1969, and began fielding his own Surtees Formula One cars in 1970.

A spirited sports car competitor as well, John co-drove the winning Ferrari at Sebring in 1963. After a bad smash in a Can-Am car late in 1965, he came back to be

the Can-Am champion in 1966, driving a Lola-Chevrolet. He has also driven a Chaparral for Texan Jim Hall (page 48).

Something of a loner, John is among the most dedicated and determined of racing drivers. He can usually be recognized in the pits by his tangle of prematurely gray hair and expression of intense concentration.

4 / Other Countries

JUAN FANGIO

Thought by many to be the best racing driver who ever lived, Juan Manuel Fangio was World Champion five times. He was born in Balcarce, Argentina, in 1911, and as a boy acquired the nickname "El Chueco" (Bow Legs) because of the way he played soccer.

His father was an Italian house painter with little money; and Juan had to go to work in the local garage when he was eleven. He first raced as a riding mechanic when he was seventeen and as a driver at the age of twenty-three. Most South American automotive events then were lengthy road races for modified stock cars; and Juan began with Model T and Ford V-8 specials, later driving Chevrolet coupes. He built and maintained his own cars with the help of townspeople; but because they could not afford the best, he did not win his first race until he was almost thirty.

After becoming well-known in Argentina, he was sent to Europe in 1948 by the Argentine Auto Club. He did not finish the only race he started on that trip, but he won six of ten Formula One races in 1949. Driving for Alfa Romeo, he came close to the championship in 1950 and won it for the first time in 1951. He won the title again in 1954 with Maserati and Mercedes-Benz, with Mercedes in 1955, and still once more in 1956 with Ferrari. In 1957, driving for Maserati again, he became champion for the fifth time, a mark that has not been equaled since. He was then forty-six, unusually old for any race driver, much less a World Champion.

Fangio retired the following season, having won twenty-four Grands Prix, and is now a businessman in Argentina. He always wore a brown crash helmet and seldom showed the slightest expression behind the wheel.

Although French cars and drivers were often winners in the early days of road racing, it has been German, Italian and British teams that have dominated the sport in more recent times. Hopeful of restoring French cars to the winner's circle, Engins Matra, a French manufacturer of missiles and space vehicles, announced a racing program in 1965. Immediately successful in F3 and F2, Matra then received a large amount of money from the French government enabling them to field a Grand Prix team in 1968.

From the beginning of the program Matra's number-one factory driver has been Jean-Pierre Beltoise, a small and wiry Parisian born in 1937. His father was a butcher, and Jean-Pierre drove a delivery truck for him before studying engineering for two years. Also an enthusiastic motorcycle racer, he was a national champion eleven times in various classes during the three years after his discharge from the French army. Trying sports car racing next, he was making a promising beginning until he was badly injured at Reims, skidding out of control on a gasoline slick. His left arm is partially paralyzed as a result; but the tough Beltoise has nevertheless persisted in his efforts to make Matra a winner.

During 1968 Ken Tyrrell campaigned an independent Matra with an English Ford engine for Jackie Stewart,

while Beltoise drove a factory car to develop the new Matra V-12 engine. In 1969 the V-12's were recalled for further improvement, and Beltoise drove a second Tyrrell Matra-Ford. Stewart won the championship easily in 1969 with the French chassis; but the factory returned the V-12 to competition in 1970 and Jean-Pierre looks forward to an all-French victory.

Jacky Ickx

The son of a well-known motoring journalist, Jacky Ickx (pronounced "eeks") was born in Brussels, Belgium, in 1945. He saw his first automobile race when he was thirteen and found it so dull that he asked his father to take him home. When he was sixteen he started racing motorcycles, becoming a Belgian champion in his first season. Not nearly as successful when he tried an automobile hillclimb, he rolled his B.M.W. sedan directly in front of a television camera. Unhurt and undaunted, he improved in further hillclimbs and progressed to sedan road racing.

Jacky raced both cycles and cars during 1965, sometimes both on the same day; and that year he won both the Belgian sedan championship and a national motorcycle title. His first season in formula cars came in 1966 when he drove F2 and F3 Matras for Ken Tyrrell.

In 1967, when he was only twenty-two, Jacky became the European Formula Two champion and also drove a Cooper-Maserati in two Grands Prix. He spent the 1968 Formula One season with prestigious Ferrari, winning his first Grand Prix at Rouen in the rain and establishing a reputation as one of the fastest F1 drivers in the wet. Shifting to the Brabham team in 1969, he was second only to champion Jackie Stewart in points at the end of the season. He returned to Ferrari for the 1970 campaign

and won the Grands Prix of Austria, Canada and Mexico, placing second in championship points once more.

An excellent long-distance sports car driver, the good-looking Ickx co-drove the winning Ford GT-40 at Sebring and Le Mans in 1969. He has said that he would also like to compete in the Indianapolis 500.

JOCHEN RINDT

Jochen Rindt was born in Mainz, Germany, in 1942. His parents were killed in an Allied bombing raid the following year, and he was raised by his grandmother in Graz, Austria. Inheriting his father's spice business, he raced his own Alfa Romeo sports cars and Brabham Formula Juniors in Austria during 1962 and 1963. He entered international Formula Two competition in 1964, also in a Brabham.

Racing in London that spring as an unknown independent, he easily defeated such stars as Graham Hill and Denny Hulme. Jochen was then signed by the British Winkelmann team and became just about unbeatable in Formula Two when driving a competitive car. He was also a co-driver of the winning Ferrari at Le Mans in 1965.

Jochen first drove an F1 car in the 1964 Austrian Grand Prix for Rob Walker and spent the next three seasons with Cooper. He joined Jack Brabham in 1968 and moved to Lotus in 1969. His first Formula One victory in six years of competition came that fall as he won the Grand Prix of the United States.

Rindt had been a controversial driver until this point. He was unquestionably one of the fastest, but some thought he had too much courage for his own good. During 1970 his driving style was much smoother, how-

ever, and he won five Grands Prix, four of them in a row.

While practicing for the 1970 Italian Grand Prix at Monza, his Lotus unexplainedly swerved into a guardrail as he braked for a curve, and he was killed. His point total was not matched during the remainder of the season, and he was named World Champion at its conclusion.

JOSEF SIFFERT

Josef Siffert, often called "Seppi" by his friends, was the leading independent Formula One driver for several seasons before joining the English March team in its first season of 1970.

Born in Fribourg, Switzerland, in 1937, he wears a red helmet with a white cross painted on its front, the national colors and symbol of Switzerland. Like many other drivers he began his racing career with motorcycles, having a difficult time of it at first because he was so poor that he had to borrow his racing leathers. He started automobile racing with a Formula Junior Lotus in 1960; and by 1961 he had already become the joint European Formula Junior champion.

He graduated to Formula One in 1962, and joined Rob Walker, the British independent owner for whom Stirling Moss once raced, in 1964. In a rare victory for an independent team, Siffert won the British Grand Prix in 1968, driving Walker's Lotus.

More successful at sports car competition than in Formula One, probably because of factory rides in the two-seaters, Jo has been a member of the German Porsche team for several seasons. He co-drove the winning Porsche at Daytona, Sebring, the Nürburgring and Zeltweg, Austria, in 1968. In 1969, when Porsche won the International Manufacturers' Championship, he

shared the winning car in six of the ten races, including the Six Hours of Watkins Glen, New York. He helped Porsche take still another championship in 1970 when he was a winning co-driver at Spa in Belgium, Zeltweg, Austria, and the Targa Florio, which is a forty-five-mile course laid out on the public roads of Sicily.

PEDRO RODRIGUEZ

Born in Mexico City in 1940, Pedro Rodriguez was already racing cars when he was fourteen years old. Too young for a license to drive on the streets of this country, he had to be driven to U.S. courses by his father in order to compete. He also raced motorcycles at an early age, winning national titles in Mexico in 1954 and 1955. When he was eighteen he drove a Ferrari in the Twenty-Four Hours of Le Mans.

Pedro was closely associated for a number of seasons with the North American Racing Team. Although NART is an independent U.S. team, its manager, Luigi Chinetti, is a Ferrari dealer in Connecticut who receives much factory support, sometimes to the extent of entering factory cars.

After thirteen years of sports car experience, including two successive victories in the Daytona Continental (1963 and 1964) for Ferrari, Pedro got his first Formula One ride with Cooper in 1967. He won the Grand Prix of South Africa that year, one of the few Formula One drivers to win a race in his first season. He drove an independent B.R.M. in 1968 and stepped up to a team Ferrari in mid-1969. In 1970 he joined the factory B.R.M. team and won the Belgian Grand Prix in June, B.R.M.'s first win in four years. That October he was leading the United States Grand Prix with only seven laps to go when

his B.R.M. ran out of gas, certainly one of Pedro's most disappointing losses.

The soft-spoken Mexican was a winner at Le Mans in 1968, co-driving a Ford GT-40. In 1970 he transferred his sports car allegiance to Ferrari's arch rival, Porsche, and won at Daytona, Brands Hatch, Monza and Watkins Glen.

5 / United States

PHIL HILL

Phil Hill is the only U.S. driver thus far to have been a World Champion. Born in Florida in 1927, he was two when his family moved to Santa Monica, California, where his father was later appointed postmaster. When Phil was nine his aunt showed him how to drive her 1918 Packard; and when he was twelve she bought him a Model T Ford. By the time he was in high school he had already owned several cars and become an expert mechanic as well.

In 1947 he left the University of Southern California for a job as a pit helper on a midget racing team. Sports cars were just then beginning to be imported into the United States, and Phil bought an MG-TC. He raced the MG in local amateur events for a while, then moved up to a Jaguar XK-120 and, eventually, a Ferrari. Through the efforts of Luigi Chinetti he was asked to

drive for the Ferrari team at Le Mans in 1955; and his international career was under way.

Phil became one of the world's best at long-distance sports car racing. He was a three-time winner at both Sebring (1958, 1959 and 1961) and Le Mans (1958, 1961 and 1962), all for Ferrari. His first Grand Prix—it was also Juan Fangio's last—was at Reims, France, in 1958. Phil was the first American to win a modern Formula One race, Monza in 1960; and in 1961 he drove a Grand Prix Ferrari to the World Championship.

Now retired from competition, Phil collects music boxes and player pianos; and he also owns a fine collection of antique and classic automobiles, many of which he has restored himself. He appears frequently on television as a commentator on road racing events.

DAN GURNEY

Lanky and personable, Dan Gurney was so popular with his many fans there was once a "Gurney for President" bumper-sticker campaign. Dan, whose father was a former opera singer, was born in Port Jefferson, New York, in 1931. He was an ardent follower of midget racing as a young boy, but switched his interest to dragging when his family moved to California. After completing his army service in Korea he bought a Triumph TR-2 and first raced on the road at Torrey Pines, California, in 1955.

His next car was a Porsche Speedster, and he did so well in it that he was given a trial in a privately owned Ferrari. Dan won three of his first six races in the big red automobile; and Luigi Chinetti arranged for his European debut in a Ferrari at Le Mans in 1958. Dan then drove a Grand Prix car for the famous Italian team during 1959, having progressed from a Triumph to Formula One in only four years. He moved to B.R.M. for 1960, drove Porsche F1 cars from 1961 until 1963, and was Jack Brabham's number-two driver in 1964 and 1965. Between 1966 and 1968 he fielded his own F1 car, the American Eagle. When he won the 1967 Belgian Grand Prix in an Eagle, he became the first American driver to win a Formula One race in an American car since 1921.

Dan has also won at Sebring (1959 with Phil Hill)

and Le Mans (1967) as well as having three victories
in the Can-Am series. Most versatile of U.S. drivers, he
was second at Indianapolis in 1968 and 1969 in an Eagle
and has won the Riverside 500 for stock cars no less than
five times. Dan retired from driving at the end of the
1970 season but continues to be an important car builder
and the manager of his own racing teams.

Mario Andretti's auto racing career is unique because he first became an outstanding track driver and then turned to road racing as well. He also differs from other U.S. racing stars in that he was born in Italy.

Mario and his twin brother Aldo were born near Trieste in 1940. They drove Formula Juniors there in their early teens; but when the family moved to Nazareth, Pennsylvania, in 1955 they had to switch to track competition. Starting with jalopy races they worked their way through midget and sprint-car events. Aldo eventually retired after two accidents, but Mario got his first Indianapolis-type ride in 1964.

Mario, who is short, slight, and apt to wrinkle his brow when he talks, won the championship of the United States Auto Club three of his first five years racing the big track cars. He was unlucky at Indy for several years, but finally won the 500 in 1969. He has also driven late-model stock cars, winning the Daytona 500 in 1967.

Remembering the road racing of his youth, Mario began fitting sports car events into his busy USAC schedule in 1965. He won at Sebring in 1967, co-driving a Ford with Bruce McLaren; and he repeated there in 1970 in a Ferrari. Offered a Formula One Lotus for the United States Grand Prix in the fall of 1968 (see photo, page 10), he surprised everyone by qualifying on the pole in

his very first F1 race. He did not finish the two Grands
Prix he entered in 1969; and he had bad luck with his
STP March in 1970. But his ability to run with the best
on the road had been clearly established, and the powerful Ferrari team signed him for the 1971 road racing
season.

JIM HALL

Tall and lean Jim Hall is from Midland, Texas. Born in 1936 to a wealthy oil family, his first racing experience came in an Austin-Healey with the amateur Sports Car Club of America. After graduating from the California Institute of Technology Jim raced larger and faster cars. He also became involved in a Dallas sports car dealership with Carroll Shelby, another well-known race driver from Texas.

Jim moved to Midland in 1961, going into partnership there with Hap Sharp, a former car customer. After Jim's rather disappointing 1963 season in Europe with the British Racing Partnership Formula One team, Jim and Hap settled down at their "Rattlesnake Raceway" to develop the famous Chaparral sports cars.

The Chaparrals, named for a fast-running bird, have featured so many unusual technical advances that Jim has been called the Tom Swift of auto racing. His radical departures from usual design include a chassis made of plastic boxes, an automatic transmission, and the use of a wing over the rear of the car to keep it on the road. His latest model, the 2J, has fans at the rear which create a vacuum under the car for even greater road holding.

Chaparral successes in this country include domination of the United States Road Racing Championship, forerunner of today's Can-Am series, in 1964 and 1965

as well as Jim and Hap's 1965 Sebring victory. The revolutionary white cars have won abroad at the Nürburgring in 1966 and Brands Hatch, England, in 1967, Phil Hill co-driving. Jim has recently concentrated on Can-Am competition and, in 1970, a Camaro team in the popular Trans-American series for small sedans.

MARK DONOHUE

Often referred to as the "Captain Nice" of racing, Mark Donohue is a clean-cut, modest Ivy Leaguer who still wears his hair short. Born in 1938, the son of a patent lawyer, he grew up in Summit, New Jersey, and graduated from Brown University in 1959 with a degree in engineering. He tried a hillclimb with his street Corvette while in college and after leaving Brown became very active in Sports Car Club of America racing. He won the SCCA national Class E championship in an Elva Courier in 1961, and both the A Sedan and Formula C championships in 1965.

Mark began his association with Roger Penske of Philadelphia in 1966 when he drove Roger's Lola-Chevrolet in the Can-Am series and finished second overall to John Surtees. The team then won the United States Road Racing Championship in both 1967 and 1968, taking six of the eight races in 1967 and five out of nine in 1968.

Penske Racing Enterprises contested the Trans-American road racing championship for small sedans during 1968; and Mark's steady driving of the factory-backed Penske Camaros was a major factor in winning the series for Chevrolet. Mark and Roger won the Trans-Am for Camaro again in 1969, then changed to American Motors in 1970. They had developed the Javelin into a strong contender by the end of the season.

Mark was a co-winner of the Daytona twenty-four-hour race in February of 1969 and first entered the Indianapolis 500 that May. Brand-new to USAC track racing, he nevertheless placed seventh and was named "Rookie of the Year." In the 1970 500, only his second time there, Mark finished an impressive second.

PETER REVSON

When Mark Donohue was racing his SCCA Elva Courier, his greatest competition came from Peter Revson in a Morgan. Peter, born in 1939, is an heir to a large cosmetics fortune. He drove Formula Junior cars in this country in the early sixties. Then in 1963 he decided that he could learn faster from the tougher European competition and he moved to England.

Peter bought a second-hand bread truck there and rebuilt it to carry his Formula Three car and also to serve as a camper in which to live. He traveled 16,000 miles in the old truck that summer alone, racing in Austria, Germany, Belgium, Holland, Denmark, Italy and France.

He continued to barnstorm the European Formula Three circuit with his own car in 1964 and also drove as the third member of the Lotus Formula Two team. Since the number one Lotus driver was then Jim Clark, Peter had a chance to learn a great deal.

He returned to this country in 1965 to run in the United States Road Racing Championship series and won five races in his class. The next season he was back on the international scene, co-driving the class-winning Ford GT-40 at Sebring and Spa, Belgium.

Peter first ran in the Trans-Am sedan series in 1967, driving a factory Cougar. In 1968 he was on the Javelin team; in 1969 he drove for Mustang; and in 1970 he

joined former rival Mark Donohue with Roger Penske to drive Javelins again.

Making his Indy debut in 1969, Peter started dead last but drove so well he finished fifth. And he would have won the first 500-miler held at Ontario, California ("Indy-West"), in 1970 except for a fouled-up pit stop. He was named top performer of the event, in any case.

Blond David Earl Savage, Jr., has been called "Swede" since he was very young; and it is likely that few of his fans would recognize him by his true name. The son of a veterinarian in San Bernadino, California, Swede was born in 1947; and he was racing quarter-midgets by the time he was nine. He was on the factory Go-Kart team when he was thirteen; and at fifteen he took up motorcycling.

Racing motorcycles professionally while in high school ended his eligibility as an all-league football player; but Swede preferred the bikes and continued to race for money after high school. While working in a cycle dealership he met Dan Gurney, also an enthusiastic rider, and became his protegé.

Farmed out in his automotive apprenticeship to the Holman-Moody shops in North Carolina, Swede first helped build Grand National Fords for the southern superspeedways, then later drove them himself—and very rapidly at that. He was recalled to Gurney's All American Racers in 1968 to drive a Can-Am McLaren.

He added Trans-Am, Indianapolis-car and Formula A (SCCA's biggest single-seaters) experience during 1969 and then became second driver to Dan on the Plymouth Barracuda Trans-Am team in 1970. When the factory cut the team back to a single car for financial

reasons, Dan showed his confidence in Swede by giving him the ride. Many auto racing experts have since agreed about Swede's ability; and most regard him as a likely superstar in the exciting seasons that lie ahead.